To:

Mommy

From:

Paulina + Emilia

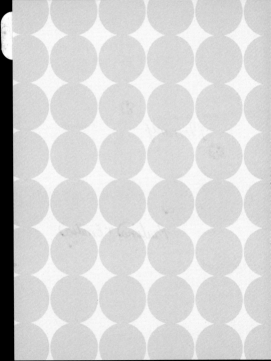

You Said It, MOM!

A Celebration of Motherhood

Written and compiled
by Ruth Cullen

Photographs by Kelly Povo

PETER PAUPER PRESS, INC.
WHITE PLAINS, NEW YORK

*For every wise and wonderful mother
out there, but especially for you, Mom*

Designed by Taryn R. Sefecka
Photographs copyright © 2004 Kelly Povo

Copyright © 2004
Peter Pauper Press, Inc.
202 Mamaroneck Avenue
White Plains, NY 10601
ISBN 0-88088-559-9
Printed in China
7 6 5 4 3 2 1

Visit us at www.peterpauper.com

You Said It, MOM!

A Celebration of Motherhood

Introduction

Since the dawn of time, mothers have been dispensing advice to their offspring in hopes of keeping them safe, happy, and healthy.

Although they had only our best interests at heart, sometimes their scare tactics left lasting impressions on our child minds ("Don't cross your eyes or they will stay that way!"), and, in our teenage years, thoroughly annoyed us ("Drink your milk," and "Don't forget to wear a hat!").

By the time we reached adulthood, however, a strange thing happened: we actually started to listen. And much to our shock and horror, we discovered that Mom was right all along.

Listen carefully as you read the following pages and, without a doubt, you will hear Mom's familiar voice ringing in your ears, uttering the very words that helped shape the person you are today.

Thanks, Mom. You were right.   *R. C.*

You said it, Mom!

If life gives you lemons, make lemonade.

Expect trouble as an
inevitable part of life and
repeat to yourself the most
comforting words of all:
This, too, shall pass.

Ann Landers

You said it, Mom!

If at first you
don't succeed, do
it the way your
mother told you to.

Cherish your human
connections: your
relationships with
friends and family.

Barbara Bush

You said it, Mom!

Sometimes
the best way to
get your point
across is to say
nothing at all.

There is right
and wrong.
Only two choices,
you choose.

Rosie O'Donnell

Exercise every day.
Remember, if you rest, you rust.

You said it, Mom!

You catch more flies with honey than with vinegar.

When love
doesn't treat you
like a lady, teach it
better manners.

Ronda Rich

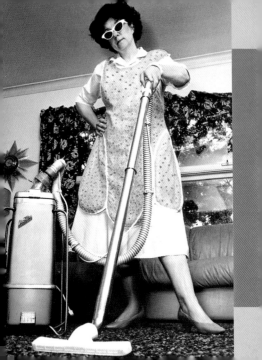

Sometimes the
best helping hand
you can get is a
good, firm push.

Joann Thomas

Be gentle and
patient with people.
Everybody's bruised.

Katie Lambert

You said it, Mom!

Be the kind of friend you wish to have.

My mother
taught me
life should be
savored, love
should be
forever,
gifts should
be from
the heart.

Sophia Loren

It's never
too late
to say you're
sorry.

People who fight fire
with fire usually
end up with ashes.

Abigail Van Buren

Growing up, my mom used to encourage me to "always have something to look forward to." Over the years, I have found that having plans and goals has helped me to keep moving forward. As I achieve goals, it gives me a sense of accomplishment and courage to set new ones.

Joan Lunden

A mistake is
simply another way
of doing things.

Katharine Graham

You can't get
spoiled if
you do your
own ironing.

Meryl Streep

Just don't give up trying
to do what you really want
to do. Where there's love
and inspiration, I don't
think you can go wrong.

Ella Fitzgerald

You said it, Mom!

You can't change the rain, but you can open an umbrella.

Never regret.
If it's good,
it's wonderful.
If it's bad,
it's experience.

Victoria Holt

You said it, Mom!

Every exit is a new beginning.

My mother wanted her
daughter to develop her own
tools of survival. To be
independent. To be Somebody.
She never doubted I could
learn anything, however difficult.
And because of her faith in me,
I never doubted it either.

Estelle Ramey

Always be a first-rate
version of yourself,
instead of a second-rate
version of somebody else.

Judy Garland

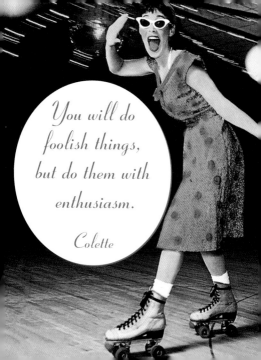

You will do
foolish things,
but do them with
enthusiasm.

Colette

Barbie is a doll,

not a goal.

Patti LaBelle

My mother drew a distinction between achievement and success. She said that achievement is the knowledge that you have studied and worked hard and done the best that is in you. Success is being praised by others, and that's nice, too, but not as important or satisfying. Always aim for achievement and forget about success.

Helen Hayes

There's no use crying over spilled milk.

You can have it all.
You just can't have
it all at one time.

Oprah Winfrey

You said it, Mom!

Actions speak
louder than
words.

Avoid junk food. You are what you eat.

Get a good
night's sleep.
Things will
look better in
the morning.

Get down on
your knees and
thank God you
are on your feet.

Irish Saying

When you come to a
roadblock, take a detour.

Mary Kay Ash

You said it, Mom!

Save your money and one day it might save you.

If you can't change
your fate, change
your attitude.

Amy Tan

When we saw the demands [our mother] placed on herself, there was no need for her to tell us that we were expected to live up to certain standards as well. And we never wanted to disappoint her.

Cokie Roberts

Life is what we
make it, always
has been,
always will be.

Grandma Moses

Don't count your chickens before they hatch.

My mother taught me all about trust—most of all, how to trust in myself. Now that I am going to be a mother, I understand what an incredible lesson that was and I want to pass that on to my child.

Catherine Bell
star of JAG

You learn
something
new every day
if you pay
attention.

Don't wish your
life away. It goes
by quickly enough.

Sharon Cullen

Pretty is as pretty does.

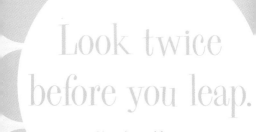

Look twice
before you leap.

Charlotte Brontë

Beyond all lessons, beyond the model she provided, my mother gave me a parent's ultimate gift: She made me feel lovable and good. She paid attention; she listened; she remembered what I said. She did not think me perfect, but she accepted me, without qualification.

Fredelle Maynard

Soup should be seen
and not heard.

E. C. McKenzie

Don't run with scissors.

Learn to enjoy
your own company.
You are the one
person you can count
on living with for the
rest of your life.

Ann Richards

Beauty comes in all colors, shapes, and sizes. Love your differences—they're what make you special.

Don't judge
a book
by its cover.

You said it, Mom!

Take a nice, hot bath and you'll feel better.

It is important to
use the gifts you have.
I know I have beautiful
eyes and I use them.

Former First Lady Mamie Eisenhower,
quoted by her granddaughter,
Susan Eisenhower

You said it, Mom!

Choose your friends wisely. You are the company you keep.

You said it, Mom!

Don't try to
please everybody—
you'll end up
pleasing nobody.

Don't burn bridges.
You never know
how many times
you'll have to cross
the same river.

Joan Lunden

Don't wait around
for other people to
be happy for you.
Any happiness you
get you've got to
make yourself.

Alice Walker

You can fool
some of the people
some of the time,
**but you can't
fool Mom.**